MW00618296

Cowboys and Cantos

New poems with revised and selected poems
from
I Come from Cowboys... and Indians and
Oklahoma Cantos

First edition, first printing
October, 2012
Durant, Oklahoma

i

Praise for *I Come from Cowboys... and Indians OklahomaCantos* and *Cowboys and Cantos*

Centered in the plains of Oklahoma, this powerful collection of poetry by Ron Wallace invites us to his country where red-tailed hawks circle a landscape made real by the grace of his writing, writing that seems to come from his soul. He is an exciting new voice in American poetry. What Grace!

> Billie Letts
> New York Times best-selling author of
> *Where the Heart Is* and *Made in The U.S.A.*
> winner of the Walker Percy and
> the Oklahoma Book Awards.

Alnilam, nearing the end of its blue period in Orion, is expected to become a red supergiant, eventually to explode as Super Nova. Fitting symbol for a poet whose cantos and poems begin solidly in good Oklahoma dirt, journey to the Kiamichis, to Wyoming and the wild ghosts of the West, then suddenly explode in the landscape of art. The lightning he notices, with his clear eye for detail, also strikes readers in a book we want to re-read and keep close at hand, like memory. Wallace is at the peak of his powers when he assures us, "There is no end, just close of day."

> Sandra Soli
> author of *What Trees Know*
> 2008 Oklahoma Book Award in Poetry

Elegiac in the best sense of the word, Ron Wallace, in Cowboys and Cantos, offers tender, dusty elegance that informs us of a rich history composing family, heroes and the poet himself into the song that is Oklahoma – a hallowed hymn for all of us here at home, a moving performance that will speak to many others as well!

Ken Hada,
author of *Spare Parts* and *The River White*
winner 2011 Western Heritage Award

In Ron Wallace's first book, *Native Son*, my father wrote in the introduction that he'd love to take even the slightest credit for making Ron a poet, but he couldn't. He also said Howard Starks and James Dickey could claim powerful influences. But I think Ron would agree with me, after five volumes of poetry, there is a piece of Dennis Letts in there. My father and mother both have written introductions to Ron's work. They called his writing "powerful, and beautiful, and sensual, and absolutely honest." Now his new collection *Cowboys and Cantos* echoes those sentiments from Texoma to Tulsa. I know Mom is proud and Dad would be too.

Tracy Letts – actor and playwright
The Man from Nebraska 2004 Pulitzer Prize finalist
August Osage County 2008 Pulitzer Prize winner
for drama

In _Oklahoma Cantos_, Ron Wallace has made poetry of Oklahoma: its landscape, its climate and clouds in various seasons, and, most importantly, its citizens. This is not the Oklahoma of show-business legend, but something much closer to the truth of the land and the experience of its people--wise, gritty, down to earth, and beautiful. These are fine poems from the heart of a true poet.

> Carl Sennhenn
> Oklahoma Poet Laureate 2001—2003
> author of _Travels Through Enchanted Woods_
> (Village Books Press, 2007)
> 2007 Oklahoma Book Award in Poetry

Ron Wallace places not a jar, but a baseball field in the middle of Oklahoma, where it becomes "the one constant" amid the shifting seasons, wild horses, and unpredictable sky. Wallace's poetry is vernacular, to be sure, but it keeps company with "Dickey, Jeffers, Komunyakaa, and Howard Starks" whose influences inflect the poet's voice with gruff yet lyrical honesty and a clarity seldom seen in contemporary poetry.

> Jeanetta Calhoun Mish
> author of _Work Is Love Made Visible_
> (West End Press, 2009)
> winner of the 2010 Western Heritage Award
> and the 2010 Oklahoma Book Award

"Wallace is not a poet of form and method; he is not overtly concerned with meter and rhythm; he puts the right word in the right place; he is a storyteller, a craftsman of narrative poetry. His voice is remarkable, homely, like that of a friend telling you a tale over a few beers as the Oklahoma sun sinks behind the trees.

Robert McDermott
Poet - (Dublin, Ireland)
author of *Beneath the Waves* (TJMF Publishing)

"Ron Wallace's poetry moves right into that soul space where music, love and the quiet secrets of the world reside. Every poem is a journey of expansion, beauty and the affirmation of life."

Brigitte London
Singer/songwriter
Untraveled Road, *Like a Phoenix* and *Thunder*.

I have come to think of Ron Wallace's life and work as a perfect expression of this prairie homeland we share and love. Our landscape is unpretentious, and not all can see its subtle beauty. Even fewer can make this land sing. Ron Wallace does just that with his words of unpretentious elegance.

Carol Hamilton
Oklahoma Poet Laureate 1995—1997
author of *Shots On* (Finishing line Press, 2008)
winner 1992 Oklahoma Book Award in poetry

Over the years a really talented writer develops his own persona on the printed page. I believe I and many others would recognize Ron Wallace's poetry no matter where we read it, even without his name on it. With Oklahoma Cantos he reinforces his unique persona as "the poet from Oklahoma". I believe younger poets will use Ron's work as a standard for which they will strive, and we will hear comments like, "This reminds me of Ron Wallace's stuff." But no one is ever going to match his ability to evoke a verbal landscape that is so pure Oklahoma that it reaches the souls of its people. I have been touched by his writing time and time again, and this new work only continues to build his status as a poet. I consider him one of the most talented new voices in American poetry.

Ken Nye
Maine Poet Laureate Nominee
author of *Searching for the Spring*
and *Clouds of Glory* (TJMF Publishing)

The words of this work will carry themselves. Ron Wallace will make you feel the pride and passion, the history and honor of this place we call home, *Oklahoma* (Red People).

Chief Gregory E. Pyle
Choctaw Nation of Oklahoma

Wallace may mean the title, _Oklahoma Cantos_, as a reference only to the book's first poem, but, in the etymological sense, all the poems in this book are Oklahoma cantos, or songs of Oklahoma. Wallace unabashedly embraces a regional approach and poetic identity. Paradoxically, it is that willingness to write in a particular place, struggling against a particular time, that gives the poems their universal appeal.

The result is a book that is ambitious enough to generate poetry that matters, but humble enough to generate poetry one actually enjoys reading. This is a delicate balance, but, like Johnny Cash, Wallace is able to walk the line. The poem I consider to be the book's finest is concerned with time, but in a way more subtle and complex than any other poem in the collection. "Learning to Speak Choctaw," is simultaneously an elegy for his father, a lament for his lost youth, a tribute to "the greatest generation," and a reminder of the great past and troubled present of a proud people. It is a profoundly moving poem, ending with the father's sad and stoic advice to his young son to "just keep throwin' the ball."

Books like _Oklahoma Cantos_ remind us of what it feels like to be from somewhere, whatever particular place we may be from. This is an accomplishment of which to be proud.

Benjamin Myers
Oklahoma Baptist University
Winner 2011 Oklahoma Book Award
author of _Elegy for Trains_

Poems in this book are the property of
Ron Wallace 2012
© All rights reserved

No part of this book may be copied, stored in a
retrieval system or duplicated in any form
without the prior written permission of the
publisher, except by a reviewer who may quote
brief passages to be printed in a newspaper,
magazine or journal.

Copyright © 2012 by TJMF Publishing
Cover Photos by Jerry Risner
Cover Design by Jim Furber

Printed and Bound in the United States By
Publisher's Graphics, LLC

ISBN Number: 098-29447-6-4
13 digit ISBN Number: 978-0-9829447-6-9
Library of Congress Number: 2012951818

TJMF Publishing

First printing October 2012

Foreword

Paul Valéry said, "A Poem is never finished, only abandoned." Now, I'm pretty sure Paul didn't know much about cowboys or American Indians, but he knew a little something about poetry.

And over the past five or six years, I've noticed myself changing and rearranging some of my earlier work so I decided to revisit a couple of my books. I mean if Paul Valery says it's okay, it must be okay; right?

So after talking it all through with Jane, my wife of thirty some odd years, depending on where you set the date, and a couple of other close friends and editors; I decided to revamp quite a few poems, little edits, line changes to establish movement and some major overhauls, creating almost new poems.

I included "Two-in-the-Morning-Train" and "Desperado" along with "I Will Look for You", "Last Day of Summer", many new Cantos and several other new works as well in hopes of creating a volume that matters.

Found some good cowboy and Indian words of wisdom to share as well, and I added them along with the old words of wisdom. Of course I kept Chris Wall, Chief Pyle and Billie Letts intros. They make me sound better than I am. Why give that up, right?

Ian Tyson said, "I don't see any point in writing bullshit." I figured he knew a little something about cowboys and Indians as well as writing poetry so I listened to him and Valery both, and I hope no bull shit is found within these words.

Ron Wallace

An Introduction –

from the Cowboy Nation - Chris Wall - CDW

"The Moon and Mexico"
The Whiskey and the Road
They sound like the hazy boundaries of the Territory
I once dwelt in for a goodly while.
I love the place. I come from it and long to return,
and will of course.

But before my ashes to soot, dust to dirt moment
I can catch a ride there in the comfort
of Ron's verse.

Back to a place on the far side of the wire.
Before Glidden's abomination
to a free range of the mind.

In my life I have found that poetry
best be enjoyed
like fine sippin' likker.

Slowly.

There is no rush here.
This volume is a world without clocks.
The sun, moon, rain, and snow
let you know the time of day, the season, even century.

That having been said, be forewarned:
The past will be your constant companion,
a shadow rider on the ridge that you
couldn't outrun, even if you pushed'er
Hell bent 'til dawn.

I come from cowboys too,
Those of Helmsville, Montana, and drunken Irish
miners from Butte.
There is a streak of melancholy that
runs through my people like the veins
of copper in hills above the Anaconda Mine
and the rills of the valleys
near the Clark Fork of the Missouri.
And so it is with this hard won
imaginary/honorary degree
from my own school of barroom philosophy
that I decree:

It is Ron Wallace's gift
and
his beautiful love for the music of language
that gets me through those nights
that are so black
you start prayin'
for the blues.

CHRIS WALL
DRIFTWOOD, TEXAS
8-15-08

An Introduction -
The Native View by Chief Gregory E. Pyle

Ron Wallace's newest book of poetry is threaded thickly with the history of Oklahomans as well as the history of the tribal peoples of this great place. I was thrilled to find the poem "Code Talkers" included in these pages. It tells the story I have so often told of late about the Choctaw men of this area who served in WWI and used their native language in coded messages to help win the "war to end all wars."

Wallace captures the Native voice of these historic men who volunteered for the United States Army in spite of the fact they were not regarded as citizens, and had not even been allowed to speak their language in the government schools. In fact it was common practice for them to be punished if heard speaking Choctaw. It was believed they needed to forget their language and speak only English. I can imagine their reaction when a commanding officer overhears them speaking in Choctaw and asks, "What language are you men speaking?"

Perhaps these two Native Americans fearing repercussions for speaking a language which came naturally to them might answer, "We are talking Choctaw, but we can speak English too." Of course the superior officer would be happy to find the Choctaws as he grasped a brilliant idea – find more men who spoke this mysterious language, conduct a brief training to turn Choctaw words into "code" such as tali meaning "ball" to mean "grenade" or iti tanampo – "bow" and use it to mean "Company".

The Army placed the Choctaw on every end of telephone lines and began sending messages. For the first time in the European Theater of WWI the Germans could not decipher the messages of the Allied Forces. This use of Native language by the Choctaw Code Talkers ended the war early saving perhaps as many as 100,000 Allied soldiers and 300,000 German soldiers. The Indian Code Talkers were so successful that their work was considered "classified" and the men were sworn to secrecy. The tactic was used again in WWII with fourteen different tribes participating, including Choctaw, Comanche and Navajos

This is one of many poems by Ron Wallace centered around the Native American peoples of our magnificent state. There is a very nice translation of the poem "Black Horse Standing" into the Choctaw language as well.

In *I Come from Cowboys… and Indians*, Wallace offers the reader an opportunity to hear the stories and share the histories of many people and many places, some that they may recognize as they read.

I can only hope you will enjoy this work as much as I have!

Chief Gregory E. Pyle
Choctaw Nation of Oklahoma
September 22, 2008

An Introduction:

I don't remember exactly when I met Ronnie Wallace, but it was somewhere in the late '70's when he was a student in an English class taught by my husband, Dennis at Southeastern Oklahoma State University in Durant, Oklahoma.

Often Dennis would share with me some of the writing his students were producing, and I frequently heard Ronnie's name. He may be Ron now, but he'll always be Ronnie to us. By the end of the semester, I knew we would meet because I was so impressed with his work.

Since that time I have been lucky enough to get to know him; his wife, Janie and their son Matthew. Wonderful people who make me feel like a beloved aunt, cousin, sister, friend --- and most importantly, a part of their family.

Dennis read, wrote and taught poetry, understanding it far more clearly than I, but he led me to an enjoyment and appreciation of poems. I remember his introduction to Ronnie's first volume of poems. Unfortunately, Dennis died a little over two years ago, leaving an empty place in my heart. But I am comforted in knowing his passion for language lives on in so many of his writing students, especially in Ronnie Wallace and his poetry.

This newest collection of Ronnie's work, _Oklahoma Cantos_, is brilliant, so I was thrilled when he sent me the manuscript to read, and petrified when he asked me to write an introduction. I feel inadequate to fully give the credit it deserves, but I will try.

As a poet, of course, he reveals much about himself and the people and places that make up his world. But the truly fine poets like Ronnie invite their readers to examine their own worlds, giving new life to lost memories and powerful emotions.

His poems have allowed me to smell again the sweet aroma of honeysuckle; brought back the sound of a night train rolling toward Texas. He's helped me to remember the touch of cicada husks, invited me to relive sleeping on a screened-in back porch, and to recall the famous Lopez tamale cart on the Square in Durant. Ahh, the taste of those tamales!

I've read and reread each poem in this new collection. Do I have a favorite? Sure. Each and Every one of them. I remember Ralph Mills' Durant Sporting Goods store too, and I remember saving wheat pennies and returning empty pop bottles for the two-cent deposit. I even pulled up a memory buried in my childhood years of finding rocks with rare shapes and colors, and tastes (yes, I tasted them too), then taking the best ones home to keep.

Oh, so many poems, so many memories – some that bring smiles, others that bring tears, but all with a brilliant clarity that gives them life.

Thank you, Ronnie, for giving me a reconnection to the map of my past.

Billie Letts

Table of Contents:

For my big brother, Floyd

Part I

My heroes have always been cowboys

"My heroes have always been cowboys and still are it seems, sadly in search of and one step in back of themselves and their slow moving dreams."
                                                    ~ Sharon Vaughn

"When I took my stand in this Cowboy Nation, I signed on for the whole duration. I ain't changing. You'll drag me out when I go."
                                                    ~ Chris Wall

"Things are all changing; the world's rearranging a time that will soon be no more. Where has a slow moving, once quick draw outlaw got to go?"
                                                    ~ Waylon Jennings

"I can't see any point in writing bullshit."
                                                    ~ Ian Tyson

"If you got to talking with most cowboys, they'd admit they write 'em. I think some of the meanest, toughest sons of bitches around write poetry."
                                                    ~ Ross Knox

"And he rides the wild horses, the same blood flows through their veins. Yes he rides the wild horses, and like the horses he'll never be tamed."
                                                    ~ Chris LeDoux

"Tonight we ride, and if we drink ourselves to death, ain't that the cowboy way to go?"
                                                    ~ Tom Russell

"We're burnin' daylight."
                                                    ~ John Wayne – The Cowboys

I Come From Cowboys...

and I don't like ties;
boots and blue jeans fit me best
      when I head out the door.
I'm carved wood, sculpted stone,
and tooled leather.
I'm green trees, blue sky, native earth
      a circling redtailed hawk.

My dad taught me how to read,
how to swing a hammer and cast a fishing line.
Mama taught me how   not what   to think.
      She said, "Keep it simple, son,
         always try to do the best you can.
This world gets complicated as it is
      without you chipping in."

Fifty years have marked me now with scars
of bent ten penny nails,
      fist fights and books of poetry

but in the end when the wind moves the grass
across my grave,
      I ask only that I rise
         on feathered wings one time
           and loose a last defiant cry
before I'm gone back into the stone
      below the dirt
         to sleep awhile.

Outlaws in Winter Pass
   (For Waylon Jennings)

Outlaws in winter pass the gate;
shadows across the moon, they move
into the night of memory
and restless dreams on saddles worn,
their horses black as ebon wood.
The silver night has called them in,
has beckoned them to ride again
where boot heels mark a leathered path
that leads to these soft stars...

   so bright beneath the Hunter's bow.

God made a sound for the lonesome, Heaven knows,
and you can hear it when a train whistle blows.
                                                    Chris Wall

Two-in-the-morning Train

August has burned the day to cinders,
and I sit in the dark
        on a worn wicker chair,
eyes trying to part the darkness,
see across five miles of forest,
        past highways to distant tracks
that carry a two-in-the-morning train.

It might as well be a ghost white
puff of smoke
        a phantom coyote's howl
                or Texas stars
lost across the Red.
It might as well be the pitch of night
before never open eyes.

It's leaving Oklahoma
        a fading echo in the ears
of fox and bobcat
prowling beneath a new black moon.
Won't be long now
before it goes the way of dragons,
moves into another midnight
and the myth of Dakota Buffalo.

Harmony

The pitch of night hangs in branches,
as Johnny Cash's low baritone is coming
through wires and speakers,
and I sit staring at the sound of rain in the dark,
unseen voices singing black harmonies
with hidden trees.

Rob McDermott, a fine Irish poet,
once told me he'd seen the Highwaymen
on stage in Dublin
     and he believed Johnny Cash to be
the voice of God
     or the Devil
         or maybe both.

I rise to feel the rumble
coming through the leather soles of cowboy boots
vibrating bone and blood,
a song of thunder summoned from the darkness
     moving through twisted tree roots
and solid earth,
shaking my wooden deck's iron foundation.

Lightning flashes across the sky from north to south,
revealing solstice night, and illuminating
a million drops of falling rain
before John's voice leaps out into the torrent
and God begins to sing.

September Song

Dad's cowboy hat hangs
under rifles on a red cedar gun rack
      behind my leather chair.

August has slipped away while I wasn't looking,
blue eyes beneath a straw brim.

In my left hand
      I hold a lawman's star
remnant of hard arms and a good man's heart,
as a grey wind presses my window pane,
remnant of a fading hurricane
flown inland
      to die on the coast of Oklahoma,

      Outside
worn heels on beat up boots
scuff September dirt where fathers walk
      leaving sign,
that only a tracker can read.

For without a trail to follow,
life is a pursuit of pieces scattered in a storm,
a whisper of dry leaves
      whirling away before a sad rain falls.

A Cowboy Sonnet

The wind wears November like an old blue coat
and sings the air into falling leaves;

it rattles branches in a turquoise sky,
whispering cool daylight into setting sun.

In the center of its autumn-ending tune,
I feel long low notes press their song into my skin,

winter music, reminding me you're gone --
a small blue flame in night that winter weaves.

I never dreamed I'd lose you,
never knew the winter stars could come undone.

Who'll bring me through December now,
lead Oklahoma's heart to springtime once again?

Wonder why the chorus is always so damned sad;
if Chris LeDoux was singing, it wouldn't feel so bad.

Bodacious
(For Clem McSpadden)

With the nod of a Stetson
nineteen hundred pounds and eight seconds
        of pure yellow hell
explode from a bucking chute

        and in less than two seconds
a cowboy flies like a shot duck,
hat, ass and boots in all directions
crashing into Cheyenne dirt.

One last buck from an angry tangle shakes
bullrope and bell
before the uncovered bull snorts his disgust
and saunters back
behind swinging steel gates.

Somewhere from a gathering of cowboys
        after one helluva wreck in Vegas,
Tuff Hedeman speaks through broken bones
and surgical pins

        The baddest bull there has ever been

And not a single soul
Even starts to think of arguing
with the black eyes and shattered face
        one of the six
                who rode the devil's back.

Between the Moon and Mexico

I'm looking for a day I left behind
    I'm looking for the place
where trail rides into sky on a moonlit night;
I'm looking for the words
to a sad, old Hank Williams song,

and another summer jumps the fence.

Wild blue phlox is blooming
    round the wrought iron railing
that guards the graves of a Choctaw Chief
and his family.

The old homeplace has fallen
leaving only standing markers of a little cemetery
beneath tall trees
where my pony and I ride through pasture grass
in the white light of stars.

I haven't found the day
nor the place where trail and moon collide
so I settle for blue phlox
    white stars
        and night-cooled pasture grass.

Just before a press of knee
signals time to go
    we pause beneath night's blackened field
and listen to a whippoorwill
sing a sad old Hank Williams song
    while September slips away on silver wisps
above rough banks that hold Red River
somewhere south of here
    between the moon and Mexico.

Horse Thief

Five decades hang like a horse thief
at the end of a gallows' rope.
The drop was short
     the ending swift
         dead without a fight.

Damn it all, just cut me down,
       pitch me in a pine box,
say your righteous words over hell-broke bones.

Before the crows can gather up a darker light
      I'll be gone.

I'll steal Time's stallion
     black as starless dark,
take back twenty years, cinch the girth strap tight.

I'll ride away with the south wind
      rising
        blowing blackness into drifts
between the broken stones
in tangled shades of shadowed night.

I'll spur the world,
race the falling hours in spinning flight
and light out to the Territories
     where shovel dirt will never find me.

Desperado

November rides in
from the east
on a blood bay mare
        iron spur rowels rattling,
Stetson black brim,
pulled low
above hard, hazel autumn eyes.

In the west
the sky is wearing bones
        a line of leafless sycamores
standing against graying day
in a time of outlaws.

And a rising crescent moon lifts the black
above not yet winter hills,
cocks the hammer back
        and buries the world
                under collapsing stars.

There's a Ring Around the Moon Tonight

There's a ring around the moon tonight;
black-hat angels fall to earth
      cast down from shrouded stars,
that claw through clouds over Oklahoma,
      West Texas
         and New Mexico.

A lightning flash in southern sky
lights up the Texas Road
      long gone, long gone,
and darkness swallows the river crossing
where fire lies buried in an outlaw's grave
      on high banks above the shallow river,
wooden marker taken by wild weeds.

There's a ring around the moon tonight;
the air is still and quiet
out beyond a nighthawk's call;
high notes rising
      lifting
         on reborn wings in flight
from ash and dirt, interred, rising
      rising
         a song to stand on stars,
stars that lie beyond the haloed ice
stars that never fall from a midnight sky,
high above an outlaw's grave.

Chain

Somewhere, centuries ago, a Scotsman
        from Clan Wallace
rose from the forge, looked across purple heather,
picked up a claymore and fought to be free
        of an English king.

In another century
        his blood flowed across an ocean,
and his flesh rode a buckskin mare
into Choctaw lands, hammering links
        of bone and steel.

Now, what lightning-split sky leads the son of a son
of a son of a Scotsman's son
        back here to the red dirt of Georgia
where a great-great grandfather was born
to forge steel into Southern swords,
hammer iron
        into sons and grandsons?

I sense him here,
here in the storm of a fire-streaked night
        come to inspect the metal
                in a family chain uncoiling back
from where it stretched taut across western land,
this Oklahoma where I am born
so far from Scotland
        so far from Georgia
                so far from where his bones now lie.

Night Rider

You can't fence years in with wire
or build stone walls to hold them back.
They move like mavericks, rough hooves
across soft earth.
Some are sharp horned
and will hook you if they can,
but most are slow and easy going.
Their drive just rolls on
until the stampede breaks across the plain.
If I weren't so damned old,
I'd saddle up my sorrel pony
and slow down their wild, headlong run;
turn the herd back to yesterday.
I'd cut the best from packed corrals,
burn a brand on my own small bunch
and move them into wide and grassy pastures
where I'd make camp among the chosen,
beneath fields of night and stars
      ride out among the horns
          and sing the world to sleep.

Ghosts of Twilight

In November
shades of twilight come early;
the greys and slate-blues before black
move quietly into the air.
        Owl-light
comes on feathered wings
between descending sun and rising quarter moon
where twining vines weave another world
briefly into this one.

The ghosts of wolves and bobcats
rise in broken shadows
        and walk
among stands of bois d'arc and blackjack
as unseen Choctaw Lighthorse slip
beneath tangled branches
searching for a spectral outlaw
riding on a stolen roan.

In this coming sheen of white stars and waxing moon,
mortality and minutes are suspended
        unbound by natural laws.
Nighthawk and cougar are almost gone.
Indian Summer of an eleventh month
lies warm
in the dying light of autumnal days.

Here the earth turns over,
takes on the tone of an old photograph
with a hundred different tints of black and white.

Charlie Russell or Frederic Remington
        would have painted this;
Chris Wall or Guy Clark
        would have written it into songs
accompanied by sad ringing strings
of an acoustic guitar,
but I am the privileged one.
        I walk within the magic
                breathe the past into my lungs
                and exhale the night.

In My Father's Books

I found his stolen words,
his voice
in pencil marks on margined pages
        echoing
like a rifle shot through trees.

And I read lines
        my father's once blue eyes
faded-grey,
held in the coming light of winter;
words from these pages
burned into him,
oils from his rough fingertips
        bled into this paper
                where he rises now.

He lives,
here... in Sackett's Brand
        and with each page turning,
he turns
        back into denim and leather;
muscles made swinging a nine pound hammer
flex beneath khaki sleeves
        and he walks away from the wreckage
                a cage of failing flesh
that tried to pen him in the final hours.

When December Comes...

winter spurs jingle in Wyoming skies
    and days drift down
the Rockies eastern ridge
into Colorado
on cool Canadian winds.

Before too long
    his big high-stepping black
will carry him along the Great Divide
bringing the cold
through Kansas and New Mexico.

From beneath a wide-brimmed Stetson
    his ice blue eyes drive
summer's heat below the broken surface,
and a biting wind whistles from behind
    popping his grey duster
        pushing him on
            eastward
over Oklahoma and Texas panhandles,
across the treeless plains
trying to find me
hiding here above Red River
    waiting for the snow.

He Was Reading Chinese...

his voice hanging like chimes
       vibrating across the Orient,
rich, full, melodic poetry.
Eastern wisdom, ancient teachings
filled the academic room
       like helium
expanding orange balloons.

PhD's applauded softly
nodding as if they understood,
       waiting for translation.

This was art;
it was impressive, beautiful
      exotic
           intellectual
              esoteric.

A handful of students
      in the back of the room
glanced at one another,
remained politely quiet and reserved,
though one did mouth,
      "WTF?"
to his friend seated in the same row.

I smiled
and glanced down at the hat
      on the empty seat beside me,
The John B. Stetson Company,
     made in the USA
         a row of seven x's.

I thought of horses, hawks
     and Oklahoma,
and despite the ancient tones,
echoing, soothing, beautiful,
I lifted my eyes up from my boots
     and knew
I was just a cowboy,
doomed to live and die,
puzzled by the art of Chinese poetry.

War Horses

Bukowski is inside-reading;
I leave him at my desk to wait
the dead of winter with whiskey and cigars
    and walk outside onto the cedar deck.
 I carry leather, stone, steel and oak with me
into the elements
    Dickey, Jeffers, Komunyakaa
and Howard Starks;
these are my war horses.
    They bleed Whitman,
sometimes in fine arterial spray,
sometimes in droplets that spatter
in bright red splotches
    and sometimes –
sometimes they seep, saturating the pages.
They speak of horses, hawks, yellow jackets
and mountain boomers,
Osage County, Buckhead and Bogalusa
    and I listen for echoes in trees and rain
beyond the empty clink of beer bottles
where unfolding black steals the sunset,
    as I lift worn western heels up
onto a low wrought iron table
to watch a changing sky
    before reading the blood.

Ring of Hammered Steel

The setting sun
    of Choctaw County
becomes a burst of blinding orange
in my rear view mirror,
and darkness tumbles
    from behind
       washing over hurtling steel
like flash flood water
chasing through once dry canyons.

And Broken Bow lies buried
in the blackness
    up ahead
just beyond my high beam lights.
Beyond that
    Arkansas
where my great grandfather's ghost
is shoeing horses
    for Isaac Parker.

A distant ring of hammered steel
drifts beneath the gallows
    slips out of Fort Smith
crosses the Ouachita Mountains
and comes echoing
    over centuries
       to rest with me
here among Oklahoma foothills.

Hartshorne, Oklahoma (April 17th 1917)
(For John William Wallace)

Your bones
lie beneath graveyard ground
where I stand on rain-wet grass
that grows above your stoneless sleep.

    And I listen...
listen for dark echoes
    the rifle fire
that summoned you nine decades ago
to lie beneath this Oklahoma soil.

Grandfather
    I have seen,
locked in sepia-toned shades of grey,
those Wallace eyes,
watching from another age.

I am the son of your son,
and I have come to find you
    not lying here in hardened earth
nor buried in arcane pages,
but living in my muscle and blood
    your heart moving my legs
to pace above your crypt.

Your eyes
looking out from that old photograph
were my father's eyes
        now they are mine
peering from beneath a wide Stetson brim
pulled low,
a trickle of rain cascading down
to the dirt above you.
Someday soon, with a few more creases,
        they will be my son's
studying the roll of dark clouds
over land where he stands
        listening for echoes.

Gifts
(Another One for Waylon)

Darkness outduels the sunset,
and night throws off a cape of grey clouds.

Coyote yips
echo across empty cattle pastures
    and the rumble of ghost trains
        move yesterday down rusted rails.

An outlaw moon rises through cottonwoods,
just south of summer
    and I remember nights,
nights beneath star-stacked Oklahoma skies,
dew, gathering on grass
    still green
before its shift to the pale fade,
crickets singing the darkness
    unwrapping the world
like a goodbye gift,
a silver locket on a silver chain of stars.

Some nights the music fades
    some nights
        the songs play on…

I heard somebody yodel and a hobo moan
    Jimmy, he dead;
        he been a long time gone

been a long time gone.

Part II

Way down yonder in the Indian Nation

"I have Indian Blood in me, but I have just enough white blood for you to question my honesty!"
~ Will Rogers

"The Indian survived our open intention of wiping them out. And since the tide turned they have even weathered our good intentions toward them, which can be even more deadly."
~ John Steinbeck

"I did not know then how much was ended."
~ Black Elk, Oglala Sioux Holy Man 1863-1950

"What is life? It is the flash of a firefly in the night. It is the breath of a buffalo in the wintertime. It is the little shadow which runs across the grass and loses itself in the sunset."
~Crowfoot – Blackfoot warrior and orator

"My land is where my dead lie buried."
~ Tasunke Witko – Crazy Horse

"Man does not weave this web of life. He is merely a strand of it. Whatever he does to the web, he does to himself."
~ Chief Seattle

"They made us many promises, more than I can remember, but they never kept but one; they promised to take our land, and they took it."
~ Red Cloud

October Rising

Diving on southbound lanes of concrete
    I see October rising.
An early morning sun lights hay bale buffalos
gathering across eastern pasture land
    as morning breaks the grey.

Summer is leaving
green strewn on both sides of the highway,
and wild flowers have rooted the season
    to this bit of Oklahoma
where mythic beasts breathe the past
in vapors of dawn.

I would have those dark round humps
sprout sturdy legs
    and the short curved horns of bison,
have them snort and paw the earth
before rolling in a herd of shaggy thunder
ripping out metal posts and barbed wire;

I would have them explode
    in a surging wave of bound grass
and baled ghosts from another century
    a hundred thousand hooves beating
tractored rows and black asphalt
back into this southern edge of the plains.

And from the back of my quick-footed pony
    hawk feathers braided in his mane,
I would watch them stampede
across disappeared ribbons of cement
and feel the earth tremble
    beneath my chasing horse.

Learning to Speak Choctaw

He rose like smoke from high grass
and weeds that had taken the alley
east of the Katy tracks
and shuffled across the gravel road
    black hair, black eyes,
a hundred creases in a dark brown face.

His brown hand lifted
as he saw my father bent under the hood
of his red Chevy.

"Halito, Leonard Wallace, chim achukma?"

His long sleeves pulled his hands back inside
khaki pockets.

Dad's head remained in the motor
    "Hello, Earl,
I'm fine. Need a ride to town?"

"Jus' walkin', Captain.
Headed for Red's, get me a hamburger
    if you spot me a quarter
'til I mow some lawns."

I stopped bouncing the rubber ball off the shed,
eyed the worn brogans on his feet,
and glanced at Dad still buried in his Chevy.

The old man looked at me and my beat up ball glove.
     "Halito, Little Wallace,
you the next, Allie Reynolds?"
I shrugged
     he grinned.
"Keep throwing that ball; you be
another Super Chief."

Dad pulled a handful of silver
from his pockets
     selected a twenty-five cent piece
and flipped it to the old Choctaw.

"Yokoke, my policeman friend.
I owe you four quarters
     I know.
          I go eat now."

He moved like tall grass in an easy wind
up the gravel road
to the railroad track and out of sight
     my eyes following in his wake.

"War and wine,
goddamned war and wine,"
     Dad melted back
into the engine;

"Throw the ball, Son,
     just keep throwin' the ball."

Chahta Ahaya Moma *

Two hundred years ago that waxing moon,
last moon of winter
    moon of snows
        was Panther Moon.
Old Jackson tried to kill the Choctaw moons
with strokes of ink and a feathered quill,
despite the debt he owed.

Pushmataha came with Choctaw warriors
and stood beside Sharp Knife in his time of war
with Red Coats,
but when time came to repay the Choctaw,
Sharp Knife turned into Jackson,
stole Tombigbee River and pushed the People
away beneath a Panther Moon.

A trail was cut of tears before their winter feet.
    Removal
        houses burning
in the wake of driven Choctaw,
farms taken, animals slaughtered
with Jackson warm and far away.

The Panther Moon began to wane.

Look up now
and you will sometimes see
among the jet plane lights and satellites
a white moon of January try to separate itself
from the darkened winter sky.
In its Choctaw heart it is still the Panther Moon;
it knows Jackson failed.

32

He may have taken rivers,
    lands
        and lives,
but in the end his word was dust,
his lies could carry him no further than his face
upon a twenty dollar bill
       and everywhere, all about his stolen land
there are many Choctaw standing,
Chahta ahaya moma, many Choctaw standing
       beneath a panther moon.

* "Chahta ahaya moma." The dedication of Carolyn
Keller Reeves' book, The Choctaw Before Removal
literally means, "Many Choctaw standing."

Black Horse Standing

I have seen the black horse standing
in tall grass,
felt the morning sun
bending sky around the hills
where Choctaw walked long ago.
Those days have passed;
they are no more.
The circling hawk is sleeping now,
waiting for his hunting song.
The sun has surrendered
to winter moon and white stars
and left the black horse standing
like a shadow in the night.

Issuba Lusa Hikia

Issuba lusa hashuk chaha hikia
ho pisa li tuk,
onnahinli hashi yat sa potoli
shutik at nanih a pakfokachi
hopaki kash Chata yat anowa tuk.
Nittak yammat atia;
himmakma iksho.
Akank abu a pakfopa yat nusi himaka,
owatta i taloa i himmona.
Hashi hashnakaya hastula micha himaka,
i nutak ia tuk
micha issuba lusa iba hikia tuk,
ninak i shotika ont kania.

"I will return to you in stone."
Crazy Horse

Tasunke Witko

* "Makocekile akan maonikin
tuweni wiyope okisniyelo."

In the hard eyes of Crazy Horse,
I have seen the past
look into July's sunlit sky.

And now, where Korczak's chisel fell
on a mountain in the Badlands,
beneath a field of silent blue,
sudden beauty lies locked inside
stark granite holding an unshod,
prancing war pony in its stone heart.

* This quote in Oglala Sioux is attributed to Tasunke Witko
when negotiating a treaty to sell Lakota holy ground in the
Black Hills. It translates roughly to: "Upon this earth that
we walk on, no one can sell it."

Wolves and Buffalo

Like angry ants white men were pouring forth
from many trails   restless   shifting.
Everywhere Lean Bear and Black Kettle looked,
they were as many as blades of grass
on summer prairies of the north,
all dressed alike   swarming.
    Alive,
        the city of towering stone
            was alive.
Even their roads were alive with man and horse
flowing in a constant stream of inconsistent motion
around the Cheyenne warriors.

They saw their people, a solitary drop of rain
in a swiftly moving thunder storm
        and knew
soon a great flood would wash them all away
in a mighty rush of pale torrents.

Here in this colossal capital of ants,
the Great Father Lincoln had come to greet them
with his sad and lonely eyes.
He brought shining silver medals
and papers which would speak, call them friends
and promise peace even as the long-knives
waged war among themselves.

Into the setting sun of eternal night,
Red People were fading as the two chiefs rode
in the belly of an iron beast back to Colorado.
    Like a distant rain they could smell disaster
in the cool, mountain air.

Numbers never lie.

A pack of ranging wolves will bring down a buffalo.

When the bluecoats came that chill October day,
Black Kettle was on the northern plains.

Lean Bear put his honored medals on
        picked up his talking papers
                and rode out to show the soldiers
Great Lincoln called him ally   not enemy.

Beneath a hail of rifle bullets,
he and horse both fell to ant hill earth,
lead ripping flesh and Lincoln's sacred pages.

Brass cartridges and powder smoke spoke louder
than the words of men,
tore Lean Bear from the unshod grey
and placed him up among the darkened stars
        to await the Cheyenne's end.

AWONINAHKU (Lean Bear)
1813-1864

Lawton, Oklahoma (February 17th 1909)
(For Geronimo & Jay Watson)

I

Life hangs on
    like tattered leaves
refusing to release a winter branch;
the last rays of the setting sun
    ricochet gold
before the black swallows the sky
    throws back its head
    and howls.

When moons fall and trees topple,
what is lost?
A century of rings and roots, hard bark
and dying branches?
    Time?

What falls
when antique fingers draw back a bowstring
from the white man's Cadillac seat?
    The "last kill"?
    A dying bull buffalo,
stumbling into the wrong century,
three red arrows jutting from its ribs?
    History?

II

February stars find an old man staggering
in plowed earth
      a drunken Apache
trying to throw his cavalry jacket
over the moon,
to slip up on the wind.

His ankle twists like the lid
off a bottle of White Port wine.

What falls then?
The shadow of an unhorsed warrior?
A grandfather, skin brown as his fallen bison
breathing in snorts of dust
      eyes blinking in the last blue sky?
A people?

Code Talkers
(For Chief Gregory Pyle)

They were Choctaw,
unrecognized even as United States citizens;
still they went off to World War I.
Only the white world is foolish enough
to believe you can make someone
"not an American" by saying it is so.

If my horse is in your pasture,
he is still my horse.
You may call him your horse
        but that will not change who he is.
He is still my horse.

They were Americans,
so they went to fight and bleed
with the 142nd Infantry.
They delivered Allied forces from the fire
with code talk
        Choctaw,
a once forbidden native tongue.

When Mitchell Bobb spoke through wires
to Ben Carterby, German ears
could never hear what grass said to trees.
Their talk sealed victory
        and then they returned
to Southeast Oklahoma
        no flags flying
                unrecognized
                        undecorated in their time.

Now the old code talkers are all gone,
only their voices sing on
across the wooded hills
and over low-lying valleys,
through blue and vacant skies,
through the blood and bones of Choctaw
standing here today.

In the closing days of World War I, fourteen Choctaw
Indian men in the Army's Thirty-Sixth Division, trained to
use their language, helped the American Expeditionary
Force win several key battles in the Meuse-Argonne
Campaign in France, the final big German push of the war.
The fourteen Choctaw Code Talkers were Albert Billy,
Mitchell Bobb, Victor Brown, Ben Caterby, James
Edwards, Tobias Frazer, Ben Hampton, Solomon Louis,
Pete Maytubby, Jeff Nelson, Joseph Oklahombi, Robert
Taylor, Calvin Wilson, and Walter Veach.

New Mexico Wind

A sharp edge of the sun glints off a tangled,
unrecognizable mass of metal
lying among the cactus on an unshouldered
slope of roadway,
and an upside down pickup truck is turned sideways
on the centerline fifty yards in front of us.

Highway 53,
a late afternoon desert wind
whips sand through pinyon-junipur
and mesquite across the blacktop
where we sit in a short line of idling cars.

Two ambulances scream past
        a fury of red and blue flashes
                howling like lobos.

In the July blue above,
a small grey hawk rides hot air currents
soundless   circling   watching.

A Zuni reservation police officer
        small, dark and leather-faced,
a hundred and fifty years ago   a warrior,
redirects traffic
away from the Arizona border up ahead.

"Thirty or forty minutes before the road will clear,"
he says into my window
with a prophet's solemn voice.
"Best to turn around and go back, up to I40."

But Jane has already seen the white bundles,
three of them, lying at roadside
      among blowing debris.

The officer-warrior sees her distress:
"Are you okay, Ma'am?"
Her welling tears choke the answer,
      turn her voice into a nod
as he fumbles for the words to ease an injured heart.
"I'm sorry you had to see…   it's bad I know."
He straightens and looks up
    into the sun
      at the circling grey.

I manage a   "Thank you, Officer"
    and reach through the open window
to shake his hand before turning the Explorer around.

In the rearview mirror
wind stirs sheets covering the dead
as if trying to free those trapped beneath the folds
    help them rise and walk   resurrected
to unknown destinations.

It is time to move on
    move on
      toward Arizona before dark
as the pale cloth rises behind us,
in a sad, delicate dance
      to the New Mexico wind.

Robert Geronimo at His Father's Grave

An old man now,
he stands before his father's grave
      swallowed by the White Man's clothes.
The long coat and blue jeans are too large,
but January comes cold to Fort Sill,
and they keep him warm beneath his cowboy hat.

He remembers his father
      sitting in St. Louis at the World's Fair,
an old man.
His creased face like tanned leather,
hair neatly cropped, parted in the middle
      selling photographs of himself for fifty cents.
For an extra dime
he neatly printed "Geronimo" on the picture.

Apache Demon, monster, murderer
sat with shoulders sagging
      under weight of a black jacket
and the twentieth century
making bows and arrows for sale to tourists.

Bullets could not kill him, but whiskey did.

Tie my horse underneath that cottonwood,
leave my saddle, my blanket
      my rifle and my bow.
In three days I will come for them.

They lay Geronimo in winter earth
with his blanket
      and his riding whip.
He did not come for his horse.

Rocks were set in cement
   piled into a pyramid;
an eagle perched on top to mark the burial spot
that would forever hold him from his home,
so Robert returned to him
   bringing Arizona deserts
      and the mountains of New Mexico
back to the grave of Geronimo.

Robert Geronimo at his father's grave in the Apache Cemetery at Fort Sill, January 13, 1964. Courtesy U.S. Army Artillery and Missile Center Museum

A Feather of the Thunderbird

I scan storm clouds rolling east,
listen for the high-pitched cry
    but no sound comes,
just a feather floating down,
down from dark, end-of-July sky
    down from clouds that threatened rain
        down to my sand and gravel drive.

Drumbeats, low and deep,
sing Thunderbird across a summer sky.
August drifts,
dappled brown with grey and white,
the feather from a great redtail
settling to earth
    token of flight,
        gift given
a gift of strength,
to mark the coming of the last
or the opening of a first.

A journey's onset always finds a destination;
endings initiates new beginnings
    and arrival marks departure.

Lightning lights the fuse of Time
    Hawk has flown.

Only rumblings of thunderdrums
    hang
in the beginning-of-ending summer air
with echoes of a feather
    floating down.

Part III

More Oklahoma Cantos

"To live in hearts we leave behind is not to die."
 ~ *Thomas Campbell - Hallowed Ground*

"Poetry is just the evidence of life. If your life is burning well, poetry is just the ash."
 ~ *Leonard Cohen*

"Who can tell the dancer from the dance?"
 ~ *William Butler Yeats*

"The past is never dead; it's not even past."
 ~ *William Faulkner*

"I grew up in this town, my poetry was born between the hill and the river, it took its voice from the rain and like the timber; it steeped itself in the forests."
 ~ *Pablo Neruda*

"A poet's autobiography is his poetry. Anything else is just a footnote."
 ~ *Yevgeny Yevtushenko*

"Poetry is a shadow asking a tree to dance."
 ~ *Carl Sandburg*

"It's surprising how much memory is built around things unnoticed at the time."
 ~ *Barbara Kingsolver - Animal Dreams*

"We do not remember days; we remember moments."
 ~ *Cesare Pavese*

Writing the Cantos

I am a writer of sentences, a narrative voice by nature so writing the cantos was a new voyage for me, a trip into a song. The sentences are still there in many places though because... because sometimes the sentences sing, but this was different.

These are not the Cantos of Pound or the metered verse of the masters. Their voices are not mine. I want to find the voice of the common man in the twenty-first century, and write for him; I want him to hear the singing of the images in our world. I want him to emerge from behind his walls, walk out into the prairies, into the rolling hills, feel the earth moving beneath his feet, smell the wildflowers that bloom everywhere and recognize this for the poetry that it is. James Dickey said, "Write what you want to say." Mark Twain said, "Write what you know." Dennis Letts once told me, "I don't have time to waste reading what doesn't interest me." These works are the result of combining all three of those ideas with my own sense of place and voice.

I never pretended to be Shakespeare, Poe, Tennyson or Longfellow. I couldn't be Dickey, Jeffers, Komunyakaa, Whitman or Howard Starks. Hell, I can't even be Ted Kooser or Guy Clark. I'm just an Okie, always will be.

I never took a pitcher's mound without intent to throw a perfect game. I never did, but now I give poetry my best shot. It won't be perfect either. Still, I try to get the voice where it needs to be so that it can be read and felt by that fellow sitting over there at the end of the bar. I like it when a cowboy buys me a beer and says,

"Yeah, that's how it is," or "Man, I remember stuff just like that." I really don't want him to wonder what the hell I meant or be concerned with my gerunds or the passive voice. It doesn't matter to me if he counts syllables in my lines or not. I just want him to feel the rhythm of the language and appreciate the weave of the words, the sound of the world.

We live in poetry. When Derek Jeter goes away from his glove hand into the hole, snares the ball, pivots, jumps and throws for the out; there it is. When a buckskin stud races the Ford up a pastured fence line, there it is again. A brown-eyed bartender hands an ice cold beer across the bar and ballads are born. There's nothing wrong with form or vocabulary that challenge a higher intellect, but there is poetry all around us, and I don't want anyone to miss it because they're pursuing a symbol or a metaphor. If the poetics simply occur, green leaves budding in spring, fine; if not, that's fine too.

The Cantos are a probably overly-ambitious undertaking intended to capture sights and sounds from the whole of 'my' Oklahoma. For me this is a poetry of place. It is filled with the land and its creatures, small pieces of a magnificent whole. I've had the pleasure to witness most of these brief scenes in the time I've spent on this spinning ball that formed me like a potter's wheel into an Okie. Chris Wall once told me that I liked to write the word "Oklahoma" as much as he liked to hear the sound of "Texas" when it rolled off his tongue. I agree. And I don't see one damned thing wrong with either of us, at least in that regard.

RonWallace
Durant, Oklahoma

Oklahoma Cantos

1

Mornings carry a chill
that holds back green sneaking through brown blades,
and ghost moons sink in eastern skies
where the edge of the sun is coming.

2

A small herd of shaggy buffalo
stands in a cattle pasture,
anachronisms, grazing on trucked alfalfa,
dreaming unwired prairies and far wider skies.

3

Steel-grey April rain washes
discarded Sonic sacks and Coca Cola cups
into muddy creeks beneath county bridges,
replacing dyed color with blue sage and yellow poppies.

4

Spring shakes out high, white clouds
to drift above farm ponds,
where snake doctors dance with cattail reeds
edging muddy waterlines.

5

Pickup trucks pulling horse trailers decorate weeds
off shoulderless roads
with carcass of armadillo and possum.
A meeting of crows darkens the new grass.

6

Oklahoma winds bend tall trees,
carry the rumbling drumbeats of early summer thunder
and hail-pounded tin roof timpani
ahead of charging darkness riding afternoon air.

7

The rising sun lights high blue fields
over mid-morning elms.
Southern breezes move honeysuckle scent
through uncut stalks of Johnson grass.

8

A barbed wire spine rusts, buried in bark
beneath a cardinal's song,
and orange-flamed Paintbrushes split coyote bones
in an empty pasture.

9

Two redtails sit on twin high line poles,
abandoned by wire and electricity.
Pilgrim mimosas march the full length
of a deserted driveway.

10

Summer is a sorrel horse
waiting to be ridden
through sways of purple ironweed, Indian Blankets
and goldenrod coloring green prairie waves.

11

Constellations roam from Kiamichi Mountains
to panhandle prairies,
crisscross trails of long dead Kiowa campfires.
Old smoke curls skyward, tempting new suns.

12

A crisp brown husk climbs a plank
of grey barn wood,
lifeless, wingless, the locust flown
somewhere into the surrounding green.

13

Four horses wander in pastured grass
beyond boot heels hooked
on the wooden rail of a summer fence
under a spiral of dappled feathers.

14

Scattered cattle stand in broken shades
of a few post oak trees
off fenced edges of black-patched two lane highway,
dusty buffalo grass burning in July heat.

15

Red dirt dust collects on dented fenders
of a '49 Ford left to rust
among blackjack oaks sprouting through
the ghost of a flathead V8.

16

A winding creek bends under remnants
of barbed wire sagging across a shallow gulley,
where fireflies appear in flashes, disappear,
and reappear in tangled vines above the ravine.

17

The long July days end in fire
rising from a western sun sinking into slate blue
as dusk unpacks stars to tack black onto night
and cool the heated air.

18

Darkness swallows the world;
the air becomes tree frogs and crickets
singing moonlight
through night branches in shining white strips.

19

Miles to the east a southbound train rolls
toward Texas
riding diamonds across the night
with a low grumble of metal.

20

August burns to a feathered ash and scatters
as September rises in the widening grey
bound to a hurricane wind
bringing cattle-cooling Gulf Coast rain.

21

A distant whistle writes lines of poetry,
to the last lightning bugs of summer
where night sky already smells like October,
slipping through torn leaves.

22

The stars of Pegasus brush approaching Autumn
onto a canvassed pitch of sky,
and falling black gathers back into blanket shape
painting the ground beneath the air.

23

Rain gathers in low black clouds,
dark herds moving across the grey sky --
rolling, changing, sputtering
in a stampede ahead of the forked lightning.

24

A grey blanket of rain hangs in the distance;
cold splotches strike powdered dirt
with plopping sounds
blackening the deep tans of dry earth.

25

Air comes alive with scorched yellow
raining in torrents on a sweep of north wind,
and a spike-antlered buck walks the fence line
of a neighbor's pasture.

26

The steel sky has lowered its weight
onto the skeletons of hickory and pecan trees
pressing sun into the ground,
burying its fire in the still blackness.

27

Green-eyed solstice sings winter
to life in flames of the shortest sun breaking
winter wide open,
drawing the cinch tighter on the year ending.

28

Cedar wreaths and silver bells,
antique stones standing in quiet cemeteries,
little towns awaiting early snows,
memories of other times.

29

Boot tracks mark the shining white,
glistening in the winter sun where
the gods stand in the sliding light of December
among unleafed trees.

30

Two scraggly black calves
behind wire in the blinding white of Oklahoma snow
pull icy tendrils from a round bale
steaming beneath dark skies of a winter's day.

31

In the hours before a new beginning
comes the sound of wings,
with the shadow of a hawk who brought
the snow of the moon to the world.

32

Old years close in flares of light,
and new ones are born bathed in blue,
days dancing like Cheyenne warriors
calling ghosts to ride with them into the fight.

33

Ice sings beneath the blue,
writing January on tall skies
in ghost white contrails
drifting among moving cumulus.

34

Alnilam, bright in the black of night,
the hunter high above,
the air cold, the world white,
and nothing moves below this light.

35

The cold has teeth and talons,
wails a banshee's song,
midnight growling February black,
wind howling outside winter walls.

36

Tufted brown feathers
bouncing like a weathered tennis ball
search for spring icy snow
behind a smoking Ford burning winter away.

37

A quarter moon burns bright
behind unleafed limbs,
clouds racing across its face ,
stampeding cattle in warm winter sky.

38

The end of snows, a March night afire
in a halo of clouds
behind leafless walnut trees standing,
sentinels on Oklahoma's edge.

39

Redbuds bloom in ragged fence rows
along dirt road section lines
mingling with perfect white dogwoods
that foretell the lengthening of days.

40

The western sun lights a circling redtail
against the blue
high above barbed wired lands, cattle
meandering through tamed grass.

41

A black and tan German Shepard sits
beneath a tall cottonwood,
patient, relaxed, awaiting
the chattering grey squirrel's descent.

43

White swirls of cloud roll, angry,
beneath a wall hanging black, spitting rain
before tree-bending gusts
a howling beast rushing to the kill.

44

Dry creek beds rush with a sudden
found force carrying leaves and broken limbs
in a temporal river
over and under the blacktop roads.

45

Tornado blackened air descends
in whipping spirals
lifting the world in dirt and debris
flinging it into oblivion.

46

Summer is pacing the horizon
like the last big cat stalking Blue River banks.
Late May nights are still cool
before the coming swelters of July.

47

Pink roses ride the wooden rails
of an east facing deck
where the sun erupted earlier burning
the morning's mist into daylight.

48

The remnants of last autumn cling
to every nook and niche of rolling ground
taken by green blades
of a new summer season.

49

The time of longer suns has begun;
a delay of stars is on us.
The white crescent illuminates the night sky
above the bloom of Venus.

50

Heat hangs like a Navajo rug
draped across an old clothes line stretching
between iron T-poles
in the open air of a June evening.

Leaving Song

In December dusk,
the hours die
like flames in a forgotten fire
under black and moonless skies.

Winter's short-sun slips
into the stillness of solstice sky
come to lie within the woods
outside my door in winter-cold quiet.

From the blackened air above,
God sings
his leaving song in flights of geese,
and soft white glimmers
through limbs of ancient oak and elm
rip the dark
into strips of grey and ebony
as my eyes search for the music
before it's gone
from my broken Oklahoma night.

Then with the chorus fading,
flying further south,
and the hard, dark night behind me,
I turn to go back inside
and sit with ghosts awhile.

At my door the leaves are falling;
a cold wild wind will come.
Sweethearts walk by together,
and I still miss someone
                    Johnny Cash

I Will Look for You

Some days I think I'm past the loss;
until a voice, a song, a sound,
a guitar's ring comes stealing down,
wrapping me like trees in Spanish moss.

I look for you in day-lit dreams,
in pink mimosa flowers,
of summer walks that once were ours,
in shadows brought by full moon beams.

I saw you once in New Orleans
just walking there, on Jackson Square
and now, I look most everywhere
to find you lost in deep dark greens,

bright reds, soft blues and purpled hues
behind unlikely walls of pain,
in whiskey mist and midnight rain;
I never know what form you'll choose.

I search the stars and skies of grey;
I watch the wind that lifts the leaves
and come to know why hearts believe
there is no end, just close of day.

Mother's Day

Had you been born to different times,
a different world, you'd have been a painter
or perhaps a poet,
but fate placed you here, an amethyst set in a brooch,
that held us all together.
You were a fryer of chickens, a maker of dolls
        a cultivator of flowers, trees and grandchildren.
You thrived in summer's heat like some exotic flower,
and with the coming of longer suns,
I feel roses and mimosas flowering into your smile.

You only hold me now in shades of black and white,
but I hold you in vivid purples, reds, deep blues,
and bright greens all around me.
I can sense you in the full moon and stars above our
Oklahoma night, feel your mother's touch
stroking my little-boy hair with soft breezes
while I stand outside amid the sleeping flowers
        alone in the darkness
                that you taught me not to fear.

They Rise from Fading Grey Paper

They rise from fading grey paper
of a photograph
     so old
it can no longer hold them.

Dad on the right, Uncle Ira on the left
     time has eaten them;
from the knees down,
their legs, taken by years,
blend into the background dissolving
     in a blur of leaves and trees.

But their faces won't fade.
They wear Steinbeck smiles,
dark hair curling from beneath their hats.
     Their jackets over bib overalls carry
eighty years into another century
where they lift up from the thirties' dirt
of Oklahoma or Texas.

Chests and shoulders hold their heads high.
Unafraid of hard times
     or hard work,
both look into the camera
grinning like Woody Guthrie
     as if they know
they will ascend from cotton fields
from fruit trees,
from the stranglehold of slave labor wages
into perfect cloudless blue
     singing,

Way down yonder in the Indian Nation...
ride my pony on the reservation.

Return
(For Dennis Letts)

The western sun is sinking
as a redtail hawk seeks to weave day's blue
into twilight grey
      a shimmer of fire reflecting
on dappled feathers.

His wings move February in slow spirals,
lift him like a child's kite
until he catches the air in a hunter's arc
      the same air that is carrying you home
beneath cold rotored-steel.

And Oklahoma rises
      rises up from its winter's ending,
reaching from the not yet green
to receive your return.

Building Radios
(For Uncle R.V.)

I watched fingers shape fire
      bend wire to move glass tubes
and free a fuse,
release electricity to climb the air,
bring Buddy Holly in from outer space.

"Not fade away, not fade away..."

Needle-nose pliers in hand,
he peered into the box he was building
at relays and circuits that formed
a hieroglyphic maze
      worked solder here
         connected copper there
and freed floating waves of Texoma
Rock n Roll.

"Not fade away, not fade away..."

When the work was done,
pieces all secured
      the radio was mine,
an uncle's gift to a sister's son,
with a silver baseball batter swinging hard
atop black plastic case, and
I clicked the dial.

"Not fade away, not fade away..."

If time and life could be rewired
into a circuit board,
I'd flip a switch and let the current flow,
snap the light back into sharp
blue eyes
    lift up legs
        and let him walk outside
feel a late May breeze
that carries music to the ears on magic waves
and washes pain away,
a nephew's gift to a mother's brother.

"Love is real, not fade away;
    love is real not fade away,
        not fade away
           not fade away…"

Hunting Golf Balls at Lake Texoma Golf Course, 1973
(For Brian Joel Remshardt)

Across the two lane blacktop
winding toward the lake
      into the Indian grass rough
and over to the soft June fairway,
we move in the black of a new moon
carrying tow sacks.
The rhythmic croak of a bull frog
calls us down the hill
from eleven's sleeping green
      to the pond's edge
where we hide summer tennis shoes,
unopened beer and a bottle of Boone's Farm
in the cattails for safekeeping.
The water is still cool,
unheated by July and August just yet
      we enter in whispers
with teenage jokes of shrinking genitals
and cautions of silence.
Trespassers here, we are unwanted,
come to steal the treasure of bad golfers.
The mud comes oozing up between our toes
as we step gently,
sweeping our hands along the bottom,
retrieving Titleists and Top Flites
until deeper water
takes our hands out of play,
forces the feet to sweep the silky muck
feeling for the hard, dimpled covers
      rolling there on the pond floor.
With each touch
we duck beneath the murky waves
bringing up balls, once lost
      to rise and fly again.

Hub Cap Bases and Left-handed Shortstops
(For Forrest Wright)

We grew up
in days of hubcap bases
    and left-handed shortstops,
in times of no catcher's mitts, no facemasks
or shinguards to buckle on.
We met on neighborhood fields
between houses that leaned with old age,
carrying bats taped and nailed,
wearing buck and a quarter gloves.
We divided in teams
according to descending ages
    and we played baseball.

No umpires lived then.
You were out when you were out
    and safe when you were safe.
The games were as certain as the sunset
spring through early fall.
One team won; the other lost
    and no one got a trophy.
Now the vacant lots are all empty,
only our ghosts gather among the weeds
paying no heed to the schedules
    or sponsored uniforms
        and scorekeepers
who have taken the playing of the game away
and turned it into work.

Hollyhock

Past a gathering of elms
off my western deck, a dense green thicket
of thorn bush and vine
      grows heavy to a row of oaks.
Hours crowd with days and weeks
weaving a web impassible as this hedged corner
of pasture-turned yard.

Blood red from the deep green tangle
      a cardinal emerges
and lights on a rusted iron spine of barbed wire
grown through a living fence post
and fifty Oklahoma summers.

His feathers bleed on the light
of a slow setting sun,
painting the ghost of a hollyhock bush
      lost across four decades.
Near a corner of storm cellar concrete
erupting from backyard earth,
it stands beside a flowering redbud tree.

Wine red blooms so dark at the center,
they appear stained black...

I feel cool linoleum beneath bare feet,
see the hummingbird nearly disappear
inside crimson petals,
hear Mom tell me not to wander off
      dinner is almost ready.

But I have already wandered
    wandered far away,
across forty falls, forty winters
to this dwindling of August
with its hurricane-cooled summer air
    far away from Mom's back porch
and that wine red hollyhock.

Highland's North Field

In days when boys walked,
a railroad twisted on creosote crossties
        and steel rails
                out of Kansas
and fell across Oklahoma into Texas
passing graveyard stones standing
beneath shading limbs of uncompromising oak
and six unmarked graves in a row.

Long before they tore out those iron-railed tracks,
we walked on the rust, throwing rocks
at antique glass insulators on rotting highline poles
        and wandered into Highland Cemetery
to read tall Woodmen of the World markers,
bearing names and dates that turned
a new century into the burying grounds
with Rebel soldiers who had outlived Appomattox,
Lee and the Confederacy.

When progress begins its slow urban sprawl
        no iron spikes can hold the past in its place;
not a railbed rock will remain,
the steel tracks and telegraph wires all disappear;
cattle pastures and pecan groves
all evolve into back yards and golf course greens,
but I sometimes wonder
if the dead don't miss the train whistle's blow
out here where six unmarked graves
still lie in a row
in the forgotten edge of an old cemetery
        sleepers that only I know.

Last Day of Summer

With the soft hum of cicadas
playing the air
like the fading strum of a Spanish guitar,
the last day of summer hangs its light
        on scattered stars
above Oklahoma,
and slips away on raven wings,
leaving September
        drifting in its wake.

In the coming light of shorter suns,
I stand alone
in a sand and gravel driveway
        watching
the last lightning bugs flicker
        living fire
                burning the season
to the ground,
turning the world over
and over again
        in the heat of summer dreams
                somewhere
off the coast of October.

Night

I am born into the night
with a flickering tongue of lightning
        miles away
and thunder so low it almost goes unnoticed
behind the distant scent of rain.

The air around me remains unlit
by the fire of yellow bulbs. I have chosen
        the dark instead,
letting it wrap me in its music
no guitar's acoustic rhythmic strumming,
only tree frogs and a coyote singing
        a dying summer.

Drifting among the elms a warm breeze finds me,
touches my skin and moves on
        like a lover slipping into shadows
beneath pitch black September leaves, blacker
still than the sky they press against.

I wish to be assimilated into the living blood of night,
        inhaled with ink black air
        and breathed across the sky,
my thoughts dripping from branches,
my eyes opening in the face of a great horned owl
        about to fly.

The Tree

Outside the eastern doors
   of this old school
      stands a tree of great age.
How many have walked beneath its limbs
like streaks of light
scattering through shade and sun
only to disappear
from its shadowed ground
and melt into
      and out of Oklahoma?

Did they sit in rows
   of wood and steel
      behind bricks and mortar,
watching winter turn to spring,
wishing to escape
the confines of this small town?

Or did they fear the ringing hammer
   of late May
that would shatter the chain
fastening them to the peanut farms
and cattle ranches
sending them into sunlight
      beyond the gnarled reach of the tree.

A Paint Pony

In denim cut to fit
the heat of Oklahoma summers,
I climbed tangled limbs of a bois d'arc
and waited the coming of ponies.
Soon, they would seek the shade
and green horse apples pebbled like cobble stones
on the ground
five feet below where I hid among thorns
and greenish-yellow leaves like a panther.

Soon I spotted the half-wild horses
rising from a slight draw below me
ascending the rolling grasses
of the field, walking to where I clung in shadows.
Two paints, a dun, and a mottled grey,
uneasy, sensing slightest movement
above them, bolted as I dropped,
but I landed aback one spotted pony,
closed my knees like a clamp,
and grabbed his black mane with both hands.

He lurched, bucking
once, twice, three, maybe four times.
I held on; and he ran,
ran faster than I had ever gone before.
I felt freedom flow in my blood,
breathed it into my lungs,
held it in the tensed muscles of youth
before relaxing my legs just a bit tired,
or over confident.

I went airborne then, landed with a tumble
through the dusty grass of July.
Brushing hair and hay blades from my eyes,
I sat up to watch the paint
disappear down a little slope ahead.

I think of this, forty years gone
stepping from my Jeep carrying a briefcase
walking toward two heavy doors
that will close behind me sealing me inside,
inside, away from the hanging limbs of bois d'arcs
and the flying hooves of a fleeing paint pony.

Once We Were Lions

Once we were lions; the world heard us roar,
    but time and tables turned.
Mantle's gone now, and Eastwood's getting old;
Woody Guthrie's guitar lies among the stars.
    Ali floats and stings no more.

Once we were gunslingers, sent to right the wrongs,
But only the ghost of Waylon Jennings
stands now at the dark end of the bar.
    Crazy Horse has turned to stone.
There's no more Camelot or King,
just a scattering of voices left with songs to sing.

Once we were the future, shining, full of dreams,
rushing headlong for the fight.
    We would be heroes, rebels with a cause.
Our flags would fly above fields of green,
beneath skies of blue
    always in the eagle's sight.

Once we were the answer
    but now we're just the question.
Those who remain are few
    our beards and hair gone grey
swords nicked and scarred along the way;
our armor's tarnished and battle-marked,
but still we mount our prancing steeds
    and rush into the fray.

Into the Mud

November winds are lifting Texas
    up across the Red.
All things green are going gold,
as life dances death
    in swirling turns
        across the yard.

A southern hymn of geese
plays in the air,
high above changing trees,
and even the rowdy chatter of crows
sounds sad and hollow
    in the late fall rain.

Endings always bother me.

Copperheads and moccasins
will be moving soon
into winter mud
to lie beneath the turning earth
    to wait for spring
and the longer light of warmer days.

Already I miss the summer music.

Embrace

February walks into my world,
this little piece of Oklahoma
that sleeps
above the shallow Red,
her ermine cape
drifting from delicate shoulders
to settle on the ground at my feet.

Beautiful dancer,
white grace sweeping through black air,
she touches my face with cool fingers,
her pearl heart gathering
on the wide brim of my Stetson.

Beneath the streetlights
the winter's night illuminates;
I extend both arms,
and accept her icy embrace,
a joining of bodies
as the music of the falling begins.

There is always poetry in snow,
a sad song in the sweet sweep of wind
moving fine powder
into the boot tracks
left behind.

Twilight in Winter

Fire no longer burns above the western rim;
air, grey as January,
slips into lungs like a Comanche.
Winter twilight in Oklahoma stands
on grass pale as hay
etching fading light between leafless limbs.

The black is coming
        coming soon
                cold and moonless
dragging a scatter of white stars
too distant
to illuminate the path
under leather Nocona soles.

The crunch of gravel
dies in the smoke of hanging breath
and stillness of walking denim.

And a brush of heavy feathers
sweeps the last light of an old year
        above drifted browns and yellows.
Darkness lands
in tree tops across the ravine,
southeast of my eyes
turning to catch the day ending.

Comes Winter to the Night

Darkness comes
screaming like a panther,
and all the gods I have abandoned
    gather in small falling flakes
and call me to the night outside the window glass,
where they swallow the streetlight
    and burn into white ash on the cold ground.

In the dark and starless December sky above
    days dance through fifty-six seasons
like drunken half breeds
and hang like tinsel on yesterday's trees.

This is how some things are meant to end,
not with Eliot's whimper
    but a sudden gust of icy wind,
head thrown back and howling,
blowing darkened light below the rattle
of black branches
    sweeping stars into crystal drifts
to be buried in winter beneath a distant dirge
of haunted highland pipes.

Owl
(For Robinson Jeffers)

He sits,
the blood of stars
dripping from shadowed branches,
    conceived in darkness
        born into night
        woven into blackness
behind a flicker of lightning
and the drumming heartbeat of thunder.

A swivel of air turns between cat-like eyes
        and a weathered barn
lit by light filtering through rough planks
into his world of leaves and branches.

Miles across fenced pastures, coyotes sing
the quarter moon to earth
        beneath his hooked feet,
and life ends in swift descent of crescent scythes,
razored talons from a godless sky.

He swallows whole in a lift of feathers
        devouring the bones of the world,
wrapping his kingdom in fur and flesh
of dying mice and rabbits.

Woodpecker

The day explodes in feathers
    falling like blue-grey snow flakes
to the retreating sound of shotgun pellets
ripping leaves,
life pitching into January air
to fall in a tangle of brown and gold.

The 410 breaks with a lift of thin smoke,
spent cartridge leaping from the iron breech
onto winter's ungrassed earth.
Trees surrounding my boots are suddenly lifeless
as I bend beneath the weight
    of vacant blue
to lift an empty brass and plastic shell.

Burnt powder perfumes icy air,
 and I lift the destroyed woodpecker in sad hands.
No blood, only death decorates his body,
smaller than a sparrow's.

He should've flown when I threw the rocks;
I would have forgiven the damage
    if he'd only taken the slightest wing,
but he had come,
come determined to knock down my western wall,
and I had come armed with steel shot.

I scoop a shallow grave
    beside a perfect elm,
next to that same wall he had attacked with such fury
    and lay the tuft of broken feathers down,
cover him
with dirt and native stone.

What remains
when Flesh and bone has run its course
    rises on acrid air with unseen wings,
and flies into winter blue
       leaving only holes
some that I will fill
    and some that I cannot.

Photo by: Ron Buck

Shooting Star

In the gusts before thunderstorms
I brace
beneath the blue-black light of summer night
        and count white flickers above Oklahoma.

Nothing compares to this air
        this light
                this world
where spirits ride the wind
ahead of quick clouds
coming like a stampede of blue roans.

From the east
        a burst of silver-blue
streaks westward,
a lone rider rushing to meet the storm,
then blackness,
a flame extinguished,
a fire
that once lit the sky above a million buffalo,
        fallen now into nothing.

When the stars themselves fall faster
        than lightning
can race above the Plains
        they whistle our short tune,
brief notes
in the grand scheme of all things.

In a Leathered Web

I've been chasing summer
since sometime last September,
but today
I snared it in a leathered web;
just reached out and caught it
as it came flickering through shade
and sunlight,
released with the whip of my son's
strong right arm
beneath the constant trees.

I Am Oklahoma

I hold the memory of my grandmother's
raven hair gone snow white.
I still see her brown skin.
She never signed Dawes' rolls
so I will never count among tribal numbers,
but I don't need a card to tell me what is true --
I am Indian.

I am this land she gave me,
fed by the rapid currents of the Arkansas
flowing into the Mississippi
through names left behind by native peoples.
I am this place,
the tumbled stones and prairie grass,
the hawk, the coyote, the buffalo.

I am the redbud and dogwood trees that flower
among the oak and elm
growing wild in thick forests.
Tangled black jacks and bois d'arcs,
these, too, are me.
I am the native stands of pecan trees,
the immigrant mimosas and chinaberries
rooted still where old home places once stood.

I am the Cimarron River where the Chisholm Trail
crossed, and Carson built his stone fort.
I am the Washita,
the blood of Black Kettle shed upon my banks.
I am the Canadian River,
northern border of the Choctaw Nation,
and the Kiamichi rushing out
of the Ouachita Mountains to join the Red

as it falls from the Texas panhandle
toward the Gulf.

I am Osage hunting here
long before this was Oklahoma or Indian Territory;
I am Chickasaw, Creek, Sac-Fox and Seminole;
I am Caddo, Kiowa and Cheyenne,
Pawnee, Apache, Comanche driven off the Plains.
I am the blood
walking into this place at bayonet point,
Choctaw and Cherokee on trails of tears.
I am Okla Humma – Red People.

In the graves of Kickingbird,
Black Beaver, Quanah Parker and Geronimo,
you will find me;
In the bones of a hundred thousand more
mixed beneath grass waves
with buffalo and unshod ponies,
I am there.
I am Hunting Horse, Dull Knife, Bacon Rind
and Sequoyah with his alphabet.
I am William Pickett, Jim Shoulders and Lane Frost,
Jim Thorpe, Mickey Mantle, Bobby Murcer
and Allie Reynolds.
I am the old ways and the new;
I am Ralph Ellison, Roger Miller, N. Scott Momaday,
evolving not disappearing;
I need no role number, no certificate of blood.
I am Native American.
I am Indian.
I am Cowboy.
I am Oklahoma.

Stones

I'm not sure when stones first spoke to me
    I was a boy,
wandering green trails,
wading shallow turns in Mineral Bayou;
and the language of stones
was a song
        drawing me to lift them
            calling me to carry them
home in faded denim pockets.

I didn't understand
    why I was compelled to lift
the small black pebble, worn smooth,
and washed onto a sand bar
beneath the hanging branches of childhood
    or the dime-sized caramel colored rock
from the dirt around third base.

I only knew
they commanded me to take them up;
    they were obsidian holding history,
clean and cool to the touch,
small enough to hold in one's mouth
like hard candy.

The flint chiseled into an arrowhead
    and freed from its wooden shaft
several hundred years ago,
whispers my name now as it did
many years ago lying in fresh-turned earth
where I walked behind Daddy's plow.

Stones still speak to me.
The polished river rocks,
tumbled to the crossing by rolling waters
have a poet's voice, mottled grey.

I pluck half a dozen more from the sand
    cast there
from where Pacific waters rush
to rocky Northern California shores,
then toss five back into the surf
    but save one for me and Oklahoma.

Fragments of a Black Hills mountain
blasted free
to reveal the face of Crazy Horse
join red brick that lined my mother's flower bed,
petrified wood from an Arizona gift shop
    and lava rocks out of the crater
of a long dead volcano in New Mexico
gather like pilgrims.

They lie on summer windowsills or sit
    like epic storytellers,
on bookshelves already holding Hemingway,
Steinbeck, Twain and Faulkner.
They speak their own words of earth and fire
    playing the air
    carrying the past
    calling me.

These rocks knew my father and grandfathers...
my great grandfathers
and their great grandfathers.
They sang to them as they have spoken to me.

I have learned the language of stones
simple as the grooves cut through them
by water, wind and time.

They have shaped worlds, shaped weapons
shaped monuments.
They have been cast up from the ocean's floor
and out of the earth's core into the light.

I have learned the language of stones
listen, they still are singing their songs.

About the Author

Ron Wallace is currently an adjunct professor of English at Southeastern Oklahoma State University in Durant where he lives with his wife, Jane. Their son Matthew is attending the University of Northern Colorado.

I Come From Cowboys… and Indians (Revisited) is Wallace's sixth book of poetry and his second book released this year after earlier releasing a baseball themed collection entitled *Hanging the Curveball*.

His first book *Native Son (American Poems from the Heart of Oklahoma)* was a finalist in the 2006 Oklahoma Book Awards. His second book was *Smoke and Stone (The Voices of Gettysburg),* and his third book *I Come from Cowboys... and Indians* won the 2009 Oklahoma Writer's Federation Best Book of Poetry Award and his fourth volume of poems, *Oklahoma Cantos* won the award again in 2011 when it was also a finalist in the Oklahoma Book Awards.

His poems have been published in Oklahoma Today, Walt's Corner of The Long Islander, Oklahoma Edge, Crosstimbers, Sugar Mule, Grandmother Earth, di-verse city anthology, Traveling Music Woody Guthrie Anthology and numerous other journals and anthologies.

He can be contacted for readings, signings or writing seminars at www.RonWallacePoetry.com, on facebook at RonWallace - Oklahoma Poetry or at www.TJMFpublishing.com.